There was no one in him; behind
his face (which even through the
bad paintings of those times
resembles no other) and his
words, which were copious, fantastic and stormy, there was
only a bit of coldness, a dream
dreamt by no one ...
History adds that before or
after dying he found himself in
the presence of God and told
Him: "I who have been so
many men in vain want to be
one and myself." The voice
of the Lord answered from
a whirlwind: "Neither am I
anyone; I have dreamt the
world as you dreamt your
work, my Shakespeare, and
among the forms in my dream
are you, who like myself are
many and no one."

THE WORLD
is made of
STORIES

David R. Loy

WISDOM PUBLICATIONS
BOSTON

Table of Contents

Preface

Those who meditate are familiar with the warnings: "Don't cling to concepts!" We should let them go because they distort our perceptions. Yet concepts in themselves are fragments, meaningful as parts of stories. The problem is not stories themselves but how we relate to them. We do not see our stories as stories because we see *through* them: the world we experience as reality is constructed with them.

That the world is made of stories is consistent with what Buddhism says about the human predicament and how it can be resolved. The foundational story we tell and retell is *the self*, supposedly separate and substantial yet composed of the stories "I" identify with and attempt to live. Different stories have different consequences. Karma is not something the self has but what the sense of self becomes, when we play our roles within stories perceived as real. As those roles become habitual, mental tendencies congeal and we bind ourselves without a rope.

If the self is made of stories, what does that imply about its death? If the world is made of stories, what does that imply about its emptiness, what Buddhism calls *shunyata*? Do our stories obscure a craving for power that underlies and motivates what we do, or is power itself a screen-story for something else? If delusion is awareness stuck in attention-traps, and enlightenment liberates awareness, does the spiritual path involve finding the correct story, or getting rid of stories, or learning to story in a new way?

In addressing these and other issues, the story that follows offers—among other things—a new way of understanding Buddhism and a new Buddhist understanding of the Way.

In the Beginning Was the Story

You get older, and you realize there are no
answers, just stories. And how we love them.

Garrison Keillor

The universe is made of stories, not atoms.

Muriel Rukeyser

Not atoms? Of course it is made of atoms. That's one of our important stories.

What other stories make our world? Creation myths; folk and fairy tales; seventeen-syllable Japanese haiku and three-day Indonesian shadow-puppet dramas; novels romantic, fantastic, and graphic; television soap operas . . . newspaper features; op-ed articles; internet blogs; talk show chatter; office memos; obituaries and birth announcements; how-to-use manuals . . . and how you're feeling this morning; what happened during our vacation; what to plan for the weekend.

A story is *an account of something*. "What's the story on these unpaid bills?"

If the world is made of stories, stories are not just stories. They teach us what is real, what is valuable, and what is possible. Without stories there is no way to engage with the world because there is no world, and no one to engage with it because there is no self.

The world is made of our accounts of it because we never grasp the world as it is in itself, apart from stories about it. We do not experience a world and then make up stories to understand it. Whenever we try to peel them all away, to discover the reality behind, whatever becomes exposed immediately transforms into story, like excavated artifacts that disintegrate as soon as uncovered.

The same is true of ourselves, but that is getting ahead of the story.

This is not to deny (or assert) that there is a world apart from our stories, only that we cannot understand anything without storying it. To understand is to story.

According to a Hindu myth, the world is upheld by the great elephant Maha Pudma, who is in turn supported by the great tortoise Chukwa.

An Englishman asked a Hindu sage what the great tortoise rests upon.

"Another turtle," was the reply.

And what supports that turtle?

"Ah, Sahib, after that it's turtles all the way down."

Stories all the way down.

Language is basically for telling stories.... A gathering of modern postindustrial Westerners around the family table, exchanging anecdotes and accounts of recent events, does not look much different from a similar gathering in a Stone Age setting. Talk flows freely, almost entirely in the narrative mode. Stories are told and disputed; and a collective version of recent events is gradually hammered out as the meal progresses. The narrative mode is basic, perhaps *the* basic product of language.

Merlin Donald

The limits of my language are the limits of my world.

Wittgenstein

The limits of my stories are the limits of my world.

Like the proverbial fish that cannot see the water they swim in, we do not notice the medium we dwell within. Unaware that our stories are stories, we experience them as the world.

But we can change the water. When our accounts of the world become different, the world becomes different.

The Greek polis was formed by warriors who came back from the Trojan Wars. They needed a place to tell their stories, because it was only in the stories that they achieved immortality. Democracy was created in order to make the world safe for stories.

Ernest Becker

Does this mean we create the world? Stories are constructs that can be reconstructed but they are not free-floating. We need stories that account for climate change and enable us to address it. We cannot simply un-story global warming—although some fossil fuel companies have tried.

> Reality is what doesn't go away when you stop believing in it.
>
> **Philip K. Dick**

We want to strip away our accounts of the world to get at the bare facts, yet "the bare facts" is an account. To try to see the-world-as-it-really-is is to enact a story.

The world is not composed of facts, because what counts as a fact is determined by the theory—the story—it is related to.

Science is not primarily about discovering facts. It is about accounting for the relationships that make them meaningful.

> Some modern moral philosophers have sought to create an ethics based on "reason alone." But when utilitarians say that ethics should be based on the consideration of the greatest good for the greatest number, they require a substantive account of the good to get started: they still need a story about the good. . . . Efforts to create a "religion within the bounds of reason alone" run up against the same problem: they end up replacing

old stories with new ones. Narrative, in short, is more
than literature; it is the way we understand our lives.

Robert Bellah

Narrative is sometimes distinguished from rationality, *mythos* from *logos*. Yet reason is a storytelling *style*, a "second-order story" that needs a story to evaluate.

That we cannot get behind our stories is not idealism, which is a philosophical claim that the world is really made of "mind stuff" rather than "physical stuff." Idealism and materialism, like rationalism, are meta-stories: stories about stories.

We want to discover the master-story, the one true meta-story that includes and explains all other stories—but it's turtles all the way up too.

The biggest meta-stories are mostly religious: God, Brahman, the Tao. Such stories try to point at something that transcends stories. Yet a meta-story cannot get outside itself to explain the relationship between stories and that-which-is-outside-stories.

A Zen metaphor warns us not to take the finger pointing at the moon for the moon itself, but "the moon itself" is also not the moon.

No dharma has ever been taught by a buddha to anyone, anywhere.

Nagarjuna

To say that we can say nothing about nirvana is to say something about nirvana.

Not-speaking may be part of a story, even as the pauses in music are part of the music. Sound need not break the silence. It can be an expression of the silence.

Do stories take place in space and time, or are place and time (in) stories? Newton's objective space and universal time is a story that ordinarily works well enough, but it cannot account for black holes or subatomic particles.

Australian dreamtime seems strange to us because we distinguish stories from places. For the aborigines places are stories: song-lines.

To "settle" a wild place means to create not only houses and farms but also the stories that make them a home. For native

Australians their deserts are home because they are verdant with stories.

To the native Irish, the literal representation of the country was less important than its poetic dimension. In traditional bardic culture, the terrain was studied, discussed, and referenced: every place had its legend and its own identity.... What endured was the mythic landscape, providing escape and inspiration.

R. F. Foster

Place-stories are essential to non-modern cultures. The more homeless stories of modernity weakened such accounts with the fiction of ownership and property—today our most basic story about place.

Landscape is a *palimpsest*: a manuscript on which more than one text has been written, with the earlier writing incompletely erased.

New Amsterdam, New York, New Jersey, New Orleans... European colonists settled the "New World" not only by expelling the "Indians" but by re-storying the land with Old World nostalgia and ambitions. As white men's guns and diseases decimated the natives, the forests and soil of the New World became defenseless against imported stories about the profits to be made in skins, timber, and crops—part of the most restless, rootless story of all, the liquefying power of money that can transform into anything you want.

Do stories alienate us from nature or embed us in it? Being natural is a role in a story. No return to an unstoried nature is possible, since such stories depend upon dissatisfaction with the un-natural alternative (civilization, technology, etc.). If there are natural people somewhere, whatever that might mean, they do not know they are natural.

Paradise is from a Persian term for an enclosed garden: *pairi* "around" + *diz* "to make [a wall]." To become aware that paradise is enclosed is to find oneself outside it.

Stories do not have sharp edges. They never begin at the beginning.

The concept of an atom is meaningful as part of a complex and still-developing story that now includes the periodic table, molecules, and subatomic particles.

The meaning of a story depends upon its context; yet that network cannot be understood without understanding the stories that compose it. I am not trapped within this hermeneutic circle because I *am* that circle. The life we are thrown into is a storied one where the task of interpretation is unavoidable and always incomplete.

Even when words remain the same, their meanings change as *we* become different—which means, as other words and stories become different. Stories are composed of other stories.

Just as a flower is made only of non-flower elements,
the self is made only of non-self elements.
Thich Nhat Hanh

A story is a point of view. There is no perspectiveless perspective. There is no way to escape perspectives except by multiplying them. A good history of America will include the viewpoints of Native Americans, African-Americans, Asian-Americans, and Hispanics. And the beaver, the buffalo, the passenger pigeon?

The sense of the world must be outside the world.
Wittgenstein

The stories that make sense of the world are part of the world. It is not by transcending this world that we are transformed but by storying it in a new way.

Or: We transcend this world by being able to story it differently.

The metaphorical nature of religious language makes its truth claims the most difficult to evaluate, because we cannot agree on what criteria to use. Myth avoids this problem by being meaningful in a different way. Religious doctrines, like other ideologies, involve propositional claims to be accepted. Myths provide stories to interact with.

According to Rollo May's *The Cry for Myth*, myths provide personal identity, ground our sense of community, undergird our moral values, and point to the inscrutable mystery of creation. We cannot outgrow myth because we cannot outgrow our need for stories that offer these.

What does our great historical hunger signify, our clutching about us
of countless other cultures, our consuming desire for knowledge,
if not the loss of myth, of a mythic home, the mythic womb?

Nietzsche

The Buddhist myth about Siddhartha's four fateful encounters with an old man, an ill man, a corpse, and a renunciate can be taken as historically factual, as an imaginative way to represent why the future Buddha left home, or as a literary device that may have nothing to do with the actual life of the Buddha yet is an effective way to story his teaching.

The polyvalence of myth is not a problem because that is how such stories work. One can respond to the myth in any of these ways—or in another way.

Theology is a branch of fantastic literature.

Jorge Luis Borges

Did Genesis begin as tales told by elders around a campfire?

Fantasy is true, of course. It isn't factual, but it is true. Children know that. Adults know it too, and that is precisely why many of them are afraid of fantasy. They know that its truth challenges,

even threatens, all that is phony, unnecessary, and trivial in
the life they have let themselves be forced into living.

Ursula K. Le Guin

In a legendary conversation with Tolkien, C. S. Lewis insisted
that myths are lies, "even though lies breathed through silver."

No, replied Tolkien: we come from God, and the myths created by us, although they inevitably include some error, "reflect
a splintered fragment of the true light, the eternal truth that is
with God." It is only through our mythmaking, in which we
become a "sub-creator" inventing stories, that we can aspire to
the perfection humans knew before the Fall.

The poetry of the mythic imagination will not, for Tolkien,
replace religion as much as *make it possible*, putting
imaginatively starved modern man once again into awed
and reverent contact with a living universe.

Randel Helms

One of the most dangerous myths is the myth of a life without
myth, the story of a realist who has freed himself from all that
nonsense.

Liberation from myth: Is that our myth?

After all, what is reality anyway? Nothing but a collective hunch. . . .
I made some studies, and reality is the leading cause of stress
amongst those in touch with it. I can take it in small doses,
but as a lifestyle I found it too confining.

Jane Wagner

Paul Tillich distinguished unbroken myth (understood to be literally true) from broken myth (no longer accepted as historically true, although still believed to have deep significance). In place of broken myth, Richard Holloway suggests "breaking open a myth." If we want to taste its fruit we need to crack the shell and chew on it.

One does not refute symbols; one *deciphers* them.

Henri Corbin

The distinction between literal and symbolic truth did not exist before the seventeenth century.

All my stories are true. Some happened
and some did not, but they are all true.

IN *Letters to a Buddhist Jew*

These things never happened, but are always.

Sallust

What is sometimes called scientism is fundamentalist because it assumes that only one kind of story is important and that the truth of such stories must be objective—in this case, verifiable by physical experimentation and subject to predictive causality. Religious and scientific fundamentalism both presuppose that all truth involves simple correspondence between a propositional claim and an observable occurrence.

Another way to evaluate a story is by its consequences when we live according to it. The most important criterion for Buddhism is whether a story promotes awakening.

She kept asking if the stories were true.
I kept asking her if it mattered.
We finally gave up.
She was looking for a place to stand
& I wanted a place to fly.

Brian Andreas

Is the universe meaningful or meaningless? Our stories make us meaning-creating beings. We are how the cosmos creates meaning.

The only secure truth men have is that which they themselves
create and dramatize; to live is to play at the meaning of life.

Ernest Becker

We play at the meaning of life by telling different stories.

We accept reality easily, perhaps because
we sense that nothing is real.

Jorge Luis Borges

A story that is interpreted for me still needs to be interpreted
by me, by what I do with it—and what it does with me.

The unconscious does not distinguish between true and untrue
stories. We are changed by those we observe.

I grow up by internalizing some of the stories that society provides: they create me and I reinforce them by acting in ways
that validate them. Stories teach me what it means to be a boy
or girl, father or son, Caucasian or Hispanic, American or Chinese, Christian or Buddhist, the importance (or not) of school
and church, the importance (rarely not) of money, including
the best ways to get it and spend it.

We accept the world we story together as "the way things
are." Yet the stories we take for granted are not the only ones
possible or the best possible, a discomforting realization easier

to evade when society is homogeneous and we are not exposed to different lifestyles, worldviews, and cultural values—to alternative stories about the world and how to live in it.

> Our truth consists of illusions
> that we have forgotten are illusions.
>
> **Nietzsche**

...stories that we have forgotten are stories.

Stories justify social distinctions. Medieval kings ruled by divine right. A Rg Veda myth about the various parts of Brahma's body rationalizes the Hindu caste system.

We challenge a social arrangement by questioning the story that validates it. When people stop believing the stories that justify the social order, it begins to change.

The dominant story of modernity has been progress. Although still hardwired into our institutions, that story has lost most of its plausibility. New genres are taking its place: apocalypse and nihilism. Apocalypse is the imminent and triumphant conclusion of our most cherished stories. Nihilism is their collapse. Both are stories about the end of stories.

Nihilism inverts progress narratives, liberating the shadow that haunted them. Losing hope in the future makes us more vulnerable to the distractions and addictions of the present—

yet this moment might be appreciated differently were we not accustomed to sacrifice it to the future.

If the world is made of stories, are its problems a result of being enthralled by—in thrall to—pernicious stories? Do violent television shows increase crime and domestic abuse? Advertising teaches us that consumerism is the way to become happy. Religious teachings can inspire institutional dogma, crusades, heresy trials...and spiritual quests.

Is the solution to such problems improved stories? Getting rid of stories? Or a better understanding of storying?

> We are between stories.
>
> **Thomas Berry**

...perhaps not a bad place to be.

A Storied Life

I can only answer the question "What am I to do?"
if I can answer the question
"Of what story or stories do I find myself a part?"

Alasdair MacIntyre

I Am Made of Stories

Stories give my life the plot that endows it with meaning. I grow up modeling myself on others who embody meaning-full stories. My character is constructed by the roles I play.

Although I play different roles in different narratives, a few become my habitual stance in the world and end up providing self-identity. It becomes difficult to alter my part in these stories. Like a car racing around and around a dirt track, the ruts deepen.

Samsara—this world of suffering, according to Buddhism— literally means "going around and around."

When Jean Genet was caught pilfering as a boy, he was told: "You are a thief!" According to Sartre's biography, that label taught Genet who he was. It provided him with the story he learned to enact.

In the long run, whatever it may be,
every man must become the hero of his own story;
his own fairy tale, if you like, a real fairy tale.

P. L. Travers

Our joys and sorrows, laughter and tears, pleasures and pains, loves and fears, epiphanies and despairs—all are storied. They are meaningful within the context of a narrative.

When I'm depressed I look for a story that makes sense of it, even if only a biochemical imbalance in the brain.

To be a person requires more than self-awareness: it involves some understanding of how I became who I am, and where I am going. Both are narrative.

Do I contradict myself?
Very well, then I contradict myself,
I am large, I contain multitudes.

Walt Whitman

If one's personality is composed of sub-personalities, each of us is composed of multiple narratives. Sometimes they work together well, sometimes not. Is what used to be called "multiple personality disorder" an extreme version of what we all experience?

What does it mean—"to make sense of life"? It simply means fitting
the elements into what I consider to be a coherent narrative. . . .
The story of my real life is not a neatly crafted story, not an
aesthetically unified, coherent novel or drama; it's something
of a hodge-podge. It's full of digression, overlapping subplots,
unfinished lines of action, trivia, changes of style and tone, dull
stretches. Yet insofar as it makes any sense at all, it can only
do so as it makes narrative sense. No other format will do.

Herbert Fingarette

Stories are not abstractions from life but how we engage with
it. We make stories and those stories make us human. We
awaken into stories as we awaken into language, which is there
before and after us. The question is not so much "What do I
learn from stories?" as "What stories do I want to live?"

Insofar as I'm nondual with my narratives, that question is
just as much, "What stories want to come to life through me?"

The unexamined life is not worth living.

Socrates

To examine my life is to reflect on my important stories.

We don't see things as they are, we see them as we are.

Anaïs Nin

The mind needs stories as much as the body needs food. There are junk stories and more nourishing ones. The food we eat becomes our bodies, assimilated stories form our identities.

When Francis Harwood, an anthropologist, asked a Sioux elder why people tell stories, he answered: "In order to become human beings." She asked, "Aren't we human beings already?" He smiled. "Not everyone makes it."

Laura Simms

When an anorexic girl looks in a mirror and sees herself as overweight, she is viewing herself within a shared social narrative about attractiveness and sexuality. A key to healing is realizing that she can change that story and her role within it.

It's hard to fight an enemy that has outposts in your head.

Sally Kempton

We do not suffer because we are in pain. We suffer because something has gone wrong with our story— wrong enough that it threatens the structure of our narration.

Peter Hershock

We are social animals because our stories need other stories, others' stories. To be bored with someone is to find their stories uninteresting. Being lonely is having no one to share stories with.

Meaning is improvised together.

> We are dependent upon each other
> for the narration of our own life-story.
> **Adriana Cavarero**

"Telling our story" is how we make sense of the world and ourselves. Some people—victims of trauma, for example—have difficulty articulating what they have experienced, yet storying and sharing the trauma can weave those threads into a stronger fabric, a more inclusive story.

> All sorrows can be borne if you put them
> in a story or tell a story about them.
> **Isak Dinesen**

Even as a personal self is constructed with stories, collective selves are constructed by remembering and enacting shared stories. During their Babylonian exile the Israelites arranged their most cherished stories into the Torah. Celebrating those narratives together kept them a people.

Other collective identities harbor memories of shameful defeat and humiliation, priming groups to re-enact them, even centuries later.

> Among animals, it's eat or be eaten.
> Among humans, it's define or be defined.
>
> **Thomas Szasz**

I live multiple stories that overlap with other stories, others' stories. A slave plays a subordinate role in his master's plot. A more egalitarian society encourages more individualistic stories as vehicles to distinguish oneself. In a caste society, you learn your place by learning your story. When class is more fluid, personal success stories jostle each other, like basketball players elbowing for the rebound.

Most attempts to individuate ourselves make us just like everyone else, but our contemporary obsession with money, fame, and romantic love did not motivate medieval peasants because those opportunities were not available. The money story cannot thrive in an economy based on self-production and barter. The fame machine cannot function without extensive communications media. The myth of romance evolved out of the plaintive songs of troubadours and the bittersweet tragedy of Tristan and Isolde. Although few of us know that story we are familiar with recent variants such as Romeo and Juliet. Falling in love is not just a biological function. Stories are necessary to process our desires and feelings.

If the self is made of stories, they are not a function of the self
but vice-versa. Did stories make us human in order to reproduce themselves? Northrop Frye said that a poet is a myth's
way of making another myth. According to Hugh Pyper, Western culture has been the Bible's way of making more Bibles. Is
civilization the way stories evolve?

With script stories attained a new means of preservation far
superior to the fragility of oral transmission. Libraries became
external repositories of collective memory. Print enabled wider
proliferation and greater security. Widespread literacy created
markets for new types of published stories such as novels,
which encouraged a more reflexive subjectivity.

We no longer obtain most of our stories from each other. We watch them on screens or listen with earphones. The celebrities we follow are more interesting than we are. Their conversation is more entertaining.

Films and television teach us that a few people are central to the plot and the rest are marginal. Main characters receive most of the attention because they are more attractive, their dialogue cleverer, their lives more exciting. Minor characters contribute to the development of their stories but they are disposable and some of them may disappear along the way.

We would like to be main characters but we have learned that the important stories are happening to other people.

At one point in cultural history we asked whether movies furnished an adequate likeness of real life. The good movies were the more realistic. Now we ask of reality that it accommodate itself to film. The good person, like the good party, should be more "movieistic."

Kenneth Gergen

In life there are no extras.

Through the wiles of television news, everything in the public sphere was now to be measured by entertainment. Or to put it another way, through television entertainment has finally escaped the news and seized life.

Neal Gabler

Because the market for television and movies is saturated, their stories must keep pushing the limits of what is acceptable in order to compete for our jaded attention. Language and images that were disturbing a decade ago are mainstream today, what is edgy now will soon become common.

> Good literature is about Love and War.
> Junk fiction is about Sex and Violence.
> **Ofer Inbar**

According to Guy Claxton consciousness is "a mechanism for constructing dubious stories whose purpose is to defend a superfluous and inaccurate sense of self." The best way for stories to secure themselves is to become part of the Master Story that is *myself*.

The main plot of the Master Story tends to revolve around fear and anxiety, because the central character can never achieve the stability and self-sufficiency that he or she craves. Hence the longing and melancholy that pervade more self-reflective stories.

> We are forever telling stories about ourselves. In telling these self-stories to others we may, for most purposes, be said to be performing straightforward narrative actions. In saying that we also tell them to ourselves, however, we are enclosing one story within another. This is the story that there is a self to tell

Ecologists tell us that the biosphere is experiencing a Great
Dying. Although half its plant and animal species may become
extinct by the end of this century, a few species are propagat-
ing exponentially: human beings of course, as well as our food
crops and favored animals (cows, pigs, chickens, dogs, cats,
etc.).

Stories with certain types of predictable plots (superheroes,
Mills & Boon) have also been proliferating. Evolutionary pres-
sures select for the most profitable ones while consigning other
varieties (contemporary poetry) to fragile ecological niches.

Myths at the heart of non-modern cultures are replaced by
invasive species that promote the cargo cult of commodifying
consumption.

Stories can exploit others parasitically or enter into symbiotic
relationship. Patriarchies maintain the moral superiority of
women and the sanctity of motherhood. Kings enforced the
authority of the medieval church, which supported the divine
right of kings.

Some stories reproduce themselves by employing threats and
promises. Chain letters warn recipients about what happened
to the last unfortunate person who did not send copies to five
friends. The Diamond Sutra declares that someone who gives

away enough alms to fill the world receives less merit than one who reads and expounds even one of its stanzas.

Other ideologies use more sophisticated strategies to protect themselves. A Marxist who challenges the official line of the day is criticized for his bourgeois tendencies. Christians who doubt the divinity of Jesus are ensnared by Satan's wiles. An analysand who questions her analyst's Freudian interpretation is resisting uncomfortable insights.

Stories can self-negate. The Diamond Sutra says that the Buddha attained nothing from perfect enlightenment, and that that non-attainment is itself perfect enlightenment.

Such paradoxes implode by defeating identification with either assertion.

What happens when I realize that my story is a story?

One meaning of freedom is the opportunity to act out the story I identify with. Another freedom is the ability to change stories and my role within them. I move from scripted character to co-author of my own life. A third type of freedom results from understanding how stories construct and constrict my possibilities.

Whether or not karma is an unfathomable moral law built into the cosmos, living a story has consequences. The difference between good and bad karma is the difference between life-stories that decrease and increase suffering. That difference is different from the difference between improving one's karma and realizing how karma works, which frees one from karma.

The most troublesome narratives attempt to secure and aggrandize an ego-self understood to be separate from the rest of the world. Its supposed interests are pursued at the cost of others. Those efforts boomerang because such a discrete self is delusory. Awakening involves realizing that "my" story is part of a larger story that incorporates others' stories as well.

Man is a make-believe animal—
he is never so truly himself as when he is acting a part.

William Hazlitt

Generations of literary scholars have been puzzled by Shakespeare, because his plays reveal so little about himself. What did he believe? What were his own stories?

There was no one in him; behind his face (which even through the bad paintings of those times resembles no other) and his words, which were copious, fantastic and stormy, there was only a bit of coldness, a dream dreamt by no one. . . . History adds that before or after dying he found himself in the presence of God and told Him: "I who have been so many men in vain want to be one and myself." The voice of the Lord answered from a whirlwind: "Neither am I anyone; I have dreamt the world as you dreamt your work, my Shakespeare, and among the forms in my dream are you, who like myself are many and no one."

Jorge Luis Borges, "Everything and Nothing"

Harold Bloom marvels that Shakespeare fashioned men and women more real than living ones, and holds Shakespeare responsible for "the invention of the human." We became modern by recognizing ourselves in his fictive selves.

Did his own lack of identity enable Shakespeare to create selves and worlds that continue to overshadow our own? "All the world's a stage, and all the men and women only players ..." His final play concludes:

> Our revels now are ended. These our actors,
> As I foretold you, were all spirits and
> Are melted into air, into thin air:
> And, like the baseless fabric of this vision,
> The cloud-capp'd towers, the gorgeous palaces,
> The solemn temples, the great globe itself,
> Yea, all which it inherit, shall dissolve
> And, like this insubstantial pageant faded,
> Leave not a rack behind. We are such stuff
> As dreams are made on...
>
> *The Tempest*

The Diamond Sutra concludes: "So should one view all of the floating world: a drop of dew, a bubble in a stream, a flash of lightning, a star at dawn, a phantom and a dream."

... but what stuff are dreams made on?

I Am Not Made of Stories

Without stories there is no self. In letting go of all stories during *samadhi* meditation I become no-thing. What can be said about this nothing? *Neti, neti*—"not this, not this." To say anything about it gives it a role in a story, even if only as a place-marker like a zero.

We love salvation stories, for example the abjection and redemption of alcoholics. "I was lost but now I'm found." When I am saved or born again or awakened, what stays the same? How do I (who?) know it's the same "I"? What provides continuity between the old self-stories and the new ones?

Am I the storyteller, or the storytold . . . or both? If sense of self is produced by stories, who is telling them?

> Does the blind man own his escort? No, neither do we the story: rather it is the story that owns us and directs us.
> **Chinua Achebe**

One becomes a person with the molding of a *persona* (Greek for "mask"). What is behind that mask? Other masks. What is behind all the masks? There is never anything behind a *persona* except another *persona*. Turtles all the way inside too.

The mask evades this truth, because it wants to be more than a mask. That there is no-thing behind all the masks is not a problem but the mask does not know this.

> To be is to mean something to someone else. This existence we cannot directly create for ourselves; it can only be given to us by another. The true human problem is this: in a sense that matters to us above everything else, we are nothing in ourselves. All we have is a profound urge to exist and the dreadful experience of non-existence.
>
> **Andras Angyal**

By doubting everything that could be doubted, Descartes believed he discovered a self-conscious mental-substance invulnerable to the body's physical transformations: a mind that persists unchanged. David Hume responded with a "bundle" theory of the self that resonates with the way Buddhism deconstructs the self: one's sense of self is composed of heaps (*skandhas*) of ever-changing mental and physical processes.

Descartes accounts for the continuity of awareness, Hume for its transformations. A narrative self—self as story—bridges the two, providing both sameness and difference. Essential to this narrative is intentionality. It is not enough to have a story about what happens. It is necessary to story *why* I do what I do.

The unity of a human life is the unity of a narrative quest.
Quests sometimes fail, are frustrated, abandoned or dissipated
into distractions; and human lives may in all of these ways also fail.
But the only criteria for success or failure in a human life
as a whole are the criteria of success or failure in
a narrated or to-be-narrated quest.

Alasdair MacIntyre

The Buddhist understanding of karma emphasizes intentionality as the key to self-transformation. The stories and roles that constitute my identity incorporate different tendencies. Spiritual development involves minimizing unwholesome motivations (greed, ill will, delusion) and reinforcing the more wholesome ones (generosity, loving-kindness, wisdom). New stories and roles are possible because I *am* that narrative and I also *am not* that narrative. I am that narrative because such stories compose my sense of self. Yet if the self were only that narrative there would be no possibility of abandoning that story and obtaining a new one. For identity to change, there must be something other than that narrative, something that is not bound by it.

Any attempt to characterize that "something other" gives it a role within my stories, yet it cannot be fixated in this way. It is not part of any particular narrative, for it is that which allows narratives to be mutable. Even describing it in this fashion pulls it into a narrative—the one you are reading right now—but anything conceptualized cannot be "it." Since it can never be identified as any-thing within a story, it always remains a non-thing, a condition of the possibility of storying.

> It is not understood by those who understand It.
> It is understood by those who understand It not.
>
> **Kena Upanishad**

The Buddhist philosopher Nagarjuna refers to *shunyata*, emptiness, as "the exhaustion of all theories and views." Those who make *shunyata* into a theory are "incurable." Reifying it into some*thing* is grasping a snake by the wrong end.

According to Kierkegaard the passion of thought is to seek for that which cannot be thought. What cannot be thought? That which thinks. What cannot be storied?

A narrative understanding of the self implies a distinction between two aspects. One's character is composed of dispositions solidified out of roles that have become habitual. This is my *identity*, from the Latin *identidem*, which means "over and over."

The other aspect of self preserves the possibility of novelty, of doing and becoming something different. This is my *no-thing-ness*. Identity is relatively fixed. *No-thing-ness* is that which cannot be fixed.

We actualize reality, without ever completing it, with stories.
Our stories are never finished; and therefore never unfinished.
If reality itself is always incomplete, each moment becomes
complete in itself, lacking nothing.

The most interesting quest narratives pursue something that is
unattainable in the way sought. In the process of questing,
however, the one who quests is transformed.

By foreclosing any closure, *no-thing-ness* transcends whatever situation one finds oneself in. I may be so caught up in stories and roles that I am unaware of my *no-thing-ness*, yet "it"
is never bound. Like a prisoner whose cell gate has never been
locked, I may not notice this freedom but insofar as I am "it"

there is never anything to attain, only something to realize and actualize.

This understanding of our double-sidedness is a key that opens many treasure-boxes.

The distinction between *identity* and *no-thing-ness* has a long pedigree both in the East and in the West, although storied in very different ways. It is the Gnostic dualism between one's divine spark and the materiality that traps it, which denigrates the material world including our physical bodies. Sartre expresses the same difference with *l'être pour soi* (being-for-itself) and *l'être en soi* (being-in-itself): I cannot *be* a waiter, I can only *play the role* of being a waiter, with or without awareness that I am only playing a role.

More recently, it is the two different aspects of personal identity in Paul Ricoeur's *Oneself as Another*: the sameness of acquired, persistent characteristics, *idem*, is contrasted with *ipse*, the mutability that holds open the possibility of change and development.

Psychotherapy distinguishes what one has become—the habitual self-narration that is problematic—and the potential to re-narrate. In understanding how one has become what one is, other possibilities arise. The "I" that becomes aware of new possibilities must be different from the congealed "me" repeating old ones. Adam Phillips describes this tension as "the conflict between knowing what a life is and the sense that a life contains within it something that makes such knowing impossible."

This distinction between "I" and "me" is fundamental to Indian and Buddhist philosophy. Being a psychological construct, the sense of self can be deconstructed and reconstructed, but the point of the spiritual path is not to get rid of the "me" (there has never been such a self, so there's nothing to get rid of) nor to get rid of all sense of "me" (which would be psychosis). Instead, the constructed sense of self becomes aware of the emptiness at its core—but that way of expressing it is too dualistic: one does not become aware of emptiness, for that emptiness is what stories and acts.

The Prajnaparamita scriptures of Buddhism describe this as the nonduality between *shunyata* (emptiness) and *rupa* (form). In terms of stories: narratives are unavoidable because they are how the world is structured and life becomes meaningful, but unless we realize our *no-thing-ness* we are trapped inside some of them—bound without a rope.

> Form is emptiness, emptiness is form.
> Emptiness is not other than form;
> form is not other than emptiness.
> **Heart Sutra**

The Indian metaphysical system of Samkhya-Yoga makes a sharp distinction between the *purusha*, which is a pure, unchanging consciousness with no attributes of its own, and *prakrti*, which is everything else. *Prakrti* is anything that can be experienced, including all stories and roles. What experiences is *purusha*, a "seer" that does nothing although its presence serves as a catalyst for the experienced world to evolve. The *purusha* mistakenly identifies with particular phenomena, especially "my" physical body and "my" mental panorama. Liberation occurs when this confusion ceases because the *purusha* / "I" realizes it is not bound by the *prakrti* / "me."

> Consciousness becomes bonded to a limited and coarse
> artificial framework through the construction of an ego-self.
> Liberation occurs when consciousness becomes
> established in its own nature.
> **Yoga Sutra**

For Advaita Vedanta, the true "I" (*atman*) identifying with the "me" (*ahamkara*) is the primary ignorance that causes suffering. The characteristics of the ego-self (the habitual stories of constructed identity) are superimposed on the "I" that is the true Self. The "I" mistakenly identifies with "my" body and possessions as well as with "my" faculties and tendencies, all of which are unreal (*maya*) and not to be confused with the immutable subjectivity of the real Self.

> He is the unseen Seer, the unheard Hearer, the unthought Thinker,
> the ununderstood Understander. Other than He there is no Seer,
> no Hearer, no Thinker, no Understander. He is your Self,
> the Inner Controller, the Immortal.
> **Brihadaranyaka Upanishad**

These various metaphysical systems are expressing the same basic realization about the difference between one's congealed *identity* and one's ineffable, unobjectifiable *no-thing-ness*. Suffering occurs because "my" *no-thing-ness* identifies with physical and mental phenomena, but no identification can be secure in an impermanent world where all phenomena arise and disappear according to conditions. Liberation occurs when I wake up to the "emptiness" of my true nature.

In terms of stories: without realizing the *no-thing-ness* that transcends all the sedimented roles in "my" stories, I remain stuck in those narratives and their consequences for good and ill. This does not mean that storying is inherently bad, although enlightenment is sometimes understood as the serenity experienced when storying ends. To see stories as the problem is to blame the victim. Instead of getting rid of stories one can *liberate* them: storying more flexibly, according to the situation. *Shunyata* "emptiness" is a heuristic device to free us from wherever we are stuck.

The only true story is "no story" and therefore one must dissolve into the one and only freedom—the ultimate nonstory— that of union with emptiness, or zeroness, or nirvana— the unconditioned vacuum of transpersonal suchness. Accepting all that I am—a fleshy, lusty, emotional, complex, vibrant self, consisting of many dimensions and identities— definitely does not fit the bill of this narrative.

Alan Clements

Samsara, this world of suffering and craving and delusion, is a pounding surf that seizes and slams us against the rocks beneath. Is salvation reaching the beach and relaxing on the sand? Or is it learning how to surf, which plays with the energy of the waves? Instead of drowning in the sea we can learn to dance with it.

The Story of Life and Death

Is death the end of my storying, or another story?

Stories are what death thinks he puts an end to.
He can't understand that they end in him,
but they don't end with him.
Ursula K. Le Guin

The oldest story, the Sumerian epic of Gilgamesh, is about his efforts to evade death. We cope with death by weaving it into stories that lessen its sting, so that it does not represent an end of life and meaning that overshadows all life and meaning.

The meaning of life is that it stops.
Kafka

If death is a wall we cannot peek over, the only way to story death is with metaphor: an undisturbed sleep, leaves falling from a tree, sailing into the sunset...

> Love and death are the great gifts that are given to us;
> mostly, they are passed on unopened.
> **Rainer Maria Rilke**

Is the problem death or our ways of storying it?

> All our knowledge merely helps us to die a more painful
> death than the animals who know nothing.
> **Maurice Maeterlinck**

We are fearful of something that always *will* happen, but there is no way to know what it is we are afraid of, thus no way to know whether we should be afraid.

> The most horrible of all evils, death, is nothing to us,
> for when we exist, death is not present;
> but when death is present, then we are not.
> **Epicurus**

Although anticipation of death can play an important role in my storying, actual death cannot. Stories about my birth (shock! pain!) and my death (terror! pain!) are different from my physical birth and death. My genesis and termination remain mysterious conditions out of which life arises and into which it returns.

> For life in the present there is no death. Death is not an event in life. It is not a fact in the world. Our life is endless, in just the same way that our field of vision has no boundaries.
>
> **Wittgenstein**

Death is only half the story. We distinguish death from life because we fear one and cling to the other, yet we cannot have one without the other: the meaning of each is the negation of the other. Awareness of either presupposes both. If life is good, and always followed by death, mustn't death be good too?

The alternatives are not life *or* death, but life-and-death *or* ...what?

> Just understand that birth-and-death is itself nirvana. There is nothing such as birth and death to be avoided; there is nothing such as nirvana to be sought. Only when you realize this are you free from birth and death.
>
> **Dogen**

I can disappear from your story, but how do I disappear from my own?

Whether or not self-*identity* dies, the goal of the spiritual path is not to attain immortality for that identity but to realize (the distinction between that identity and) my *no-thing-ness*.

Is *no-thing-ness* subject to death?

Questions about an afterlife tend to assume the same binary choices: either "I" am annihilated or "I" survive in some fashion. When the Buddha was asked what happens to an awakened person after death, he did not reply because there is something wrong with the question. For the "I" to die, it must previously have been alive. Do those categories apply to my *no-thing-ness*?

If life and/or death is a story, what traction can the fate of that story have on that which cannot play a role in any story? Anything that can be experienced will pass away, but what about a non-thing? If it is incorrect to say that my *no-thing-ness* survives death, it is equally incorrect to say that my *no-thing-ness* does not survive, since both answers make the same category mistake.

This is not an argument for postmortem survival. Insofar as "I" am a non-thing, I cannot die because I was never born.

> The whole world has taken the wrong way,
> for they fear nonexistence, while it is their refuge.
> **Rumi**

The Buddhist terms most commonly used to story *shunyata*—that which cannot be storied—are *unborn, uncreated,* and *unproduced.* The Heart Sutra declares that all things are *shunya* because they are "not created, not annihilated, not impure and not pure, not increasing and not decreasing." There is no death and no end to death.

> When you dwell in the Unborn itself, you're dwelling
> at the very wellhead of Buddhas and patriarchs.
> **Bankei**

According to Buddhism our basic problem is not death but ignorance of this unborn. If it is our essential nature, why is it so difficult to realize? The unborn is ungrounded, in the sense that there is nothing to grasp and no one to grasp it. The freedom that comes from understanding how I story and how to re-story is also the ultimate insecurity. Being storyless in itself, *no-thing-ness* is also meaningless. We gravitate toward the refuge of determinate roles within predictable narratives (including Buddhist ones). We crave the comfortable, ready-made meanings that such stories provide, which objectify a world where we know what is important and what we are meant to do. Realizing that our stories and meanings are *shunya* is a burden greater than most of us are prepared to bear. It is easier to pretend that the stories we enact together are fixed and that the roles we play are real. But then the *dukkha* suffering they create also becomes real.

The Power of Story, the Story of Power

It is not man who is impotent in the struggle against evil, but the power of evil that is impotent in the struggle against man. . . . Human history is not the battle of good struggling to overcome evil. It is a battle fought by a great evil to crush a small kernel of human kindness. But if what is human in human beings has not been destroyed even now, then evil will never conquer.

Vasily Grossman

Even if we are present at some historic event,
do we comprehend it—can we even remember it—
until we can tell it as a story?

Ursula K. Le Guin

Myth as history, history as myth. Premodern people lived in a mythic world, but how much of our own history is mythological? Although the past makes us what we are, what we have become determines what we are able to see in our history.

History often resembles "Myth," because
they are both ultimately of the same stuff.

Tolkien

... stories.

...how do we know the difference?

Is time merely a neutral grid for storying, or does its structure give meaning to what happens? The basic temporal framework of modernity has been progress: how much better we are making the world. The future will redeem the past, which is a weight to be overcome.

Premodern societies usually idealized the past, being more concerned about how far we have fallen or may fall. When history is cosmology, time and what happens in time are not distinguished. The Golden Age is not to be constructed but renewed by repetition. The future is not promise of novel possibilities but a discomforting challenge to be incorporated into the pattern. For the Maya and Aztecs, the end of time, which might occur without constant sacrifices to keep the sun-deity on its heavenly course, would be the greatest possible catastrophe.

What men believe to be true is true in its consequences.
Alfred North Whitehead

The expectation of Christ's imminent return transformed how the early Christians lived. Money, fame, power—what do those matter in light of the apocalypse that is about to change everything? There is no motivation to secure oneself in a world about to end.

The second coming of Christ was anticipated all the more eagerly when the printed Bible became available in the vernacular, revealing to everyone our collective denouement in the final Book of Revelation. No other story has done more to create the modern world.

The Reformation would not have happened if ordinary people had not convinced themselves that they were actors in a cosmic drama plotted by God: that in the Bible he had left them a record of His plans and directions as to how to carry them out...They changed the way that their world worked because they were convinced that this visible world was the least important part of the divine plan.
Diarmaid MacCulloch

Millenarianism is a story about the tension between our fallen world and its sacred source, which will soon be resolved, when the transcendent intercedes to redeem this world. Modern preoccupation with progress required only a slight modification:

the Golden Age would not be outside history but within it. This was provided by Joachim of Fiore (1135–1202), whose interpretation of Revelation became "the most influential prophetic system known to Europe until Marxism" (David Noble). The Age of the Spirit, which Joachim expected to occur soon, would be an earthly paradise.

> In modern times, this notion of advancement along a time line still prevails, except that technology has replaced religion as the force that propels events to succeed one another; nonetheless, the doctrine remains teleological.
>
> **Damian Thompson**

Modern belief in progress is a secularized version of Christian apocalypticism.

> With every passing hour our solar system comes forty-three thousand miles closer to globular cluster M13 in the constellation Hercules, and still there are some misfits who continue to insist that there is no such thing as progress.
>
> **Ransom K. Ferm**

Pro-gress is "walking forward" . . . toward what? Can there be progress if we don't know our destination?

Progress might have been all right once,
but it has gone on too long.

Ogden Nash

The growth of freedom is the central story of history, according to Lord Acton, because it represents God's plan for humanity. We trace the origins of Western civilization back to the Greek liberation of reason (philosophy) from myth, and cherish the progressive development of religious freedom (the Reformation), political freedom (the Age of Revolution), economic and civil freedom (the class struggle), colonial independence (beginning with the U.S.), psychological freedom (psychotherapy), sexual and gender freedom (women's liberation, gay rights), and so on. Freedom continues to be acclaimed as the paramount value of the West and its greatest gift to the rest of the world. Does this progression have a goal? What could complete freedom be?

Such a development is meaningful only in relation to a particular type of self-story: the individual freeing himself or herself from external determination. If we are not external to each other, however, there can be no such individual. I can never feel free enough when that is my supreme value.

The underside of progress, the shadow that haunts it, is nihilism. It appears when we can no longer believe in the narratives that reassured us before. Nihilism is the always-threatening collapse of our most important stories.

Nihilism deludes by pretending to be the end of delusion: *this* is the way things really are, without illusions. "Life has no meaning" is not the end of storying but the revenge of a repressed story.

> Man would rather will nothingness than not will.
>
> **Nietzsche**

We would rather have a story about nothingness and meaninglessness than have no story.

In medieval Europe a God story was enforced by Church and State. In the seventeenth century men killed each other *en masse* because they could no longer agree on its details. Since neither side could eliminate the other, that argument eventually yielded to more secular stories involving absolute monarchs, capitalism, and scientific control over the conditions of our existence. In the aftermath of revolutions, nationalistic narratives became dominant: one sacrificed oneself for the glory of France, or defending the Russian homeland.

> Nationalism is not the awakening of nations to self-consciousness:
> it invents nations where they do not exist.
>
> **Ernest Gellner**

The nation-state system replaced the authority of the Papacy and the Holy Roman Empire with a new type of story that deified an idealized collective self-image.

> Forgetting is a crucial factor in the creation of a nation.
> **Ernest Renan**

Remembering is crucial for awakening from nationalism.

> The struggle of man against power is
> the struggle of memory over forgetting.
> **Milan Kundera**

...the struggle to remember the stories that empower us against power.

> What criticism can do is awaken students to the mythology that lies
> behind the ideology in which their society indoctrinates them.
> **Northrop Frye**

In place of a few enforced pre-modern narratives, today we sink or swim in a tsunami of stories unleashed by freedom of the press and technologies of mass communication. How do all these stories compete, cooperate, evolve, infiltrate and subvert each other? Does social order require minimum deference to a common story? What stories are we willing to die for?

> Printer's ink has been running a race against gunpowder these many, many years. Ink is handicapped, in a way, because you can blow up a man with gunpowder in half a second, while it may take twenty years to blow him up with a book. But the gunpowder destroys itself along with its victim, while a book can keep on exploding for centuries.
>
> **Christopher Morley**

A profusion of stories is liberating yet uncomfortable, because we want to tuck ourselves securely into the True Story, the one that reveals the way things really are and what's really important.

> Ideology is the assumption that since the beginning and end of history are known there is nothing more to say. History is therefore to be lived out according to the ideology.
>
> **James Carse**

Slaves in the United States were not usually allowed to learn to read.

What Orwell feared were those who would ban books.
What Huxley feared was that there would be no reason to ban a
book, for there would be no one who wanted to read one.
Orwell feared those who would deprive us of information.
Huxley feared those who would give us so much that we
would be reduced to passivity and egoism.
Orwell feared that the truth would be concealed from us.
Huxley feared the truth would be drowned in a sea of irrelevance.
Orwell feared we would become a captive culture.
Huxley feared we would become a trivial culture....
Orwell feared that what we hate will ruin us.
Huxley feared that what we love will ruin us.

Neil Postman

Orwell feared those who would ban stories except for the
Official One. Huxley feared that there would be no reason to
ban them, for no one would want anything but entertainment
from them.

The twentieth century has been characterized by three
developments of political importance: the growth of democracy;
the growth of corporate power; and the growth of propaganda
as a means of protecting corporate power against democracy.

Alex Carey

Propaganda is to a democracy
as violence is to a dictatorship.
William Blum

Totalitarianism: only one story is permitted. Propaganda: an official story is maintained by persuading people that it is the correct one—or rather, that it is reality itself. The ultimate power is the ability to control awareness, in which case you don't need to control what people do.

The world is ruled by force, not by opinion;
but opinion uses force.
Pascal

What story manipulates those who manipulate the official story?

How do wars start? Politicians lie to journalists,
then believe what they read in the newspapers.
Karl Kraus

The story of history as the history of story. If the world is made of stories, their development is more important than the rise and fall of empires. A society's stories are conditioned by the technologies available to produce and reproduce them. An oral tradition preserves myths and fables, sometimes elaborated into epics. Kings employ bards to sing their praises and immortalize their exploits. When script externalized language, religious doctrine became more important than ritual. Print created new forums for scientific interaction, as well as newspapers and journals promoting the civil society that grew out of coffeehouses, where men gathered to discuss the latest news.

Print enabled widespread literacy and a more textual self. Literature supplements and supplants traditional sacred stories. The novels of Austen and Dickens transform those who enter into them, by exploring the consequences of character and motivation. *The Death of Ivan Ilyich* does not preach about the inevitability of death. Instead, Tolstoy gives us an extraordinary story about the life and death of an ordinary man. Fiction provides a way to learn from the life-choices of others, offering what Ricoeur calls laboratories for moral experimentation.

Every reader, as he reads, is actually the reader of himself. The writer's work is only a kind of optical instrument he provides the reader so he can discern what he might never have seen in himself without this book. The reader's recognition in himself of what the book says is the proof of the book's truth.

Marcel Proust

If we are saved not by accepting the truth of spiritual stories but in being changed by them, then the novel and its siblings offer an alternative to sacred scripture, or a new version thereof.

> Why shouldn't the truth be stranger than fiction?
> Fiction, after all, has to make sense.
> **Mark Twain**

"Good versus evil" is a simple and comfortable story. Since there is no good without a corresponding evil, I become good by struggling against that evil. Without a Devil, God stories lose their drama.

War is exhilarating because we are united against the bad guys over there.

> War is a cowardly escape from the problems of peace.
> **Thomas Mann**

Our identities are constructed from what we detest as well as what we love.

It's not enough to hate your enemy. You have to understand
how the two of you bring each other to deep completion.

Don DeLillo

We prefer the orientation of a moral code, even when we don't
follow it, to the disorientation of life without one. Morality
stories help us make sense of the world and offer a handle on
what happens to us.

"There is no good and evil, there is only power,
and those too weak to seek it."

Lord Voldemort

Rejecting God requires a God. Atheism is a theistic heresy in
the same way that Marxism is a capitalist heresy. The meaning
of a heresy depends upon the orthodoxy it rejects.

Being unable to make what is just strong,
we have made what is strong just.

Pascal

What is distinctive about modernity is not rationality but rationality in service of power: instrumental reason, especially technological development and bureaucratic organization.

Each new power won by man is a power over *men* as well. Each advance leaves him weaker as well as stronger.

C. S. Lewis

O'Brien to Winston: "The Party seeks power entirely for its own sake. We are not interested in the good of others; we are interested solely in power. Not wealth or luxury or long life or happiness; only power, pure power. . . . The German Nazis and the Russian communists came very close to us in their methods, but they never had the courage to recognize their own motives. They pretended, perhaps they even believed, that they had seized power unwillingly and for a limited time, and that just round the corner there lay a paradise where human beings would be free and equal. We are not like that. We know that no one ever seizes power with the intention of relinquishing it. Power is not a means; it is an end. . . . The object of power is power. Now do you begin to understand me?"

George Orwell, *1984*

The more control the Party has, the more it craves. Dissidents such as Winston are necessary but not because they are a threat.

When all rebels have been eliminated, other non-conformists must be found. Power without resistance becomes meaningless.

Although power seeks challenges to exercise itself against, it does not exist for the sake of anything else. When there is no goal, the means itself—more and more of the same—becomes the goal.

> Force is as pitiless to the man who possesses it, or thinks
> he does, as to its victims. The second it crushes, the first
> it intoxicates. The truth is, nobody really possesses it.
> **Simone Weil**

Buddhist sutras describe the monarchs of the Buddha's time as "intoxicated with power."

> Where belief in the omnipotence of physical force
> gets the upper hand in political life, this force takes
> on a life of its own, and proves stronger than
> the men who think about using force as a tool.
> **Albert Einstein**

Tolkien's Frodo cannot use the Ring because it would use him. To fight against power using the same means is power calling forth power. War does not determine who is right, only who is left. That is why no one wins a war, and how the Nazis won World War II (Borges, "Deutsches Requiem").

What I want is power.

Kiss 'em one day and kick them the next.

**Press baron Lord Beaverbrook
to Rudyard Kipling**

Like Northcliffe or Beaverbrook, Rupert Murdoch loved
the naked exercise of power. "That's the fun of it, isn't it?
Having a little smidgeon of power."

Anthony Sampson

According to Nietzsche our *will to power* is exposed when stories such as good versus evil are stripped away. Or is preoccupation with power based on another delusive story? Does power extend all the way down, like turtles, or does something else motivate that obession?

I put for a general inclination of all mankind, a perpetual and
restless desire of Power after power, that ceases only in Death.

Thomas Hobbes

Nietzsche believed that *we have killed God*. Darwinian evolution left religious morality vulnerable. It was only a matter of time until it fell victim to another story.

According to Darwinism life is a struggle for survival and reproductive success. Social Darwinism provided a more up-to-date principle to live by—or a more up-to-date way to rationalize how one lived. By no coincidence it appealed most to the most powerful.

One advantage of that ideology is that you needn't feel guilty about the losers you trample on your way to the top. It's a jungle out there.

Money is condensed, liquified power, "an institutionalized dream that everyone is having at once" (Weston LaBarre).

We try to fill up the hole at our core—the sense that *something is missing*, that *I am not real enough*—by becoming more wealthy, famous, attractive . . . more powerful. Power—the ability to impose my stories—offers the promise of reality. How could I be unreal, if I'm the one who decides what happens?

Is a Buddhist story better than Nietzsche's will-to-power story, better than a social Darwinist story? How does one decide among them?

> Power corrupts, and absolute power corrupts absolutely.
>
> **Lord Acton, on the Papacy**

As a religious institution propagates the founder's teachings, it becomes increasingly difficult to distinguish the best interests of his (rarely her) message from the best interests of the institution. Surely worldly success reflects the truth and value of its doctrines? I give content to my own *no-thing-ness* by identifying with a collective story that transcends me.

Preoccupation with power can also be challenged by religious teachings—in fact, a spiritual perspective provides the strongest critique, since it offers another way to address the ungroundedness of our *no-thing-ness*.

The most successful missionary religions became the religion of an empire. Empires need *universalist* stories that can unify the diverse peoples they subjugate, and *portable* stories less dependent on local shrines. Empires need religions that emphasize scriptures.

> Writing transforms religion as it transforms everything.
> The universal religions are precisely those whose deities
> reside not in idols or temples but in texts.
> **Roger Scruton**

With script words assume a life of their own and the possibility of immortality. The earth is not sacred in Abrahamic religions but God's Word is. Moses banished the golden calf by substituting two tablets. Idolatry was supplanted by bibliolatry.

The Buddha, like Socrates and Jesus, wrote nothing.

We Sioux spend a lot of time thinking about everyday things...
We see around us many symbols that teach us the meaning of life.
We have a saying that the white man sees so little, he must see
only with one eye. See a lot that you no longer notice.
You could notice if you wanted to, but you are usually too busy.
We Indians live in a world of symbols and images where the
spiritual and the commonplace are one. To you symbols are
just words, spoken or written in a book. To us they are part of nature,
part of ourselves—the earth, the sun, the wind and the rain, stones,
trees, animals, even little insects like ants and grasshoppers.

Lame Deer

Having learned to find meaning in words, we miss the meaning of everything else.

The universe story is the quintessence of reality. We perceive
the story. We put it in our language, the birds put it in theirs,
and the trees put it in theirs. We can read the story of the
universe in the trees. Everything tells the story of the universe.
The winds tell the story, literally, not just imaginatively. The story
has its imprint everywhere, and that is why it is so important
to know the story. If you do not know the story, in a sense
you do not know yourself; you do not know anything.

Thomas Berry

Is power a screen-story for fear?

It is not power that corrupts but fear. The fear of losing power corrupts those who wield it, and fear of the scourge of power corrupts those who are subject to it.

Aung San Suu Kyi

Our deepest fear is rooted in a compulsion to secure what cannot be secured.

Power is one of the oldest philosophical problems, because it challenges the rule of reason. In Plato's *Republic* Thrasymachus argues that justice is really nothing but power. Justice is what the strong do: their will becomes the law, might makes right, and the weak conform because they must. Socrates replies that if the weak can bond together to stop a tyrant, then they are the strong. That silences Thrasymachus, but Glaucon wants proof that it is better to be just than unjust, that the just man is happy and the unjust man unhappy. Socrates responds with a famous analogy between harmony in the soul and in the state. One's life is harmonious and happy when reason rules desires and emotions. A state is harmonious and just when philosopher-kings rule merchants and warriors.

Today we are critical of Plato's authoritarianism and dubious about a hierarchy that enthrones reason over the other faculties. Yet his insight remains important: craving for power reveals a defect in the soul.

The devil took Jesus to the summit of a mountain and tempted him with all the world's kingdoms. "I will give you authority over all these things, if you will worship me." Jesus responded: "It is written: worship only the Lord your God, and serve only Him." Worship power and all power will be given to you—and you will end up serving power. Jesus will serve only God.

If the devil is power, what is God?

> You must be emptied of that with which you are full,
> so you may be filled with that whereof you are empty.
> **Augustine**

A sage told Siddhartha's father that his son would become either a world-conquering king or a world-renouncing buddha. His father did everything possible to insulate him from awareness of illness, old age, and death—and when Siddhartha eventually encountered them he was so shocked that he renounced his patrimony and disappeared into the forest. According to this legend he too rejected the worldly power that was offered to him. Both Jesus and the Buddha established communities that were physically powerless and dependent upon the good will of others.

The Sangha founded by Shakyamuni was originally a motley crew of wandering mendicants, with few possessions except robes and sharing bowls. The Buddha sent them out in all directions to preach the Dharma "for the good, for the benefit of many."

Jesus charged his apostles to go out and preach that "the Kingdom of Heaven is at hand." "Take nothing for your journey, no staff, nor bag, nor bread, nor money, and do not have two tunics." The Sermon on the Mount tells us not to lay up treasures on earth. "Do not be anxious about your life, what you shall eat or drink, nor about your body, what you shall put on.... Consider the lilies of the field, how they grow; they neither toil nor spin, and yet your heavenly Father takes care of them."

What were both saying? Let go of your fears about yourself: just do your best spreading the word and have faith that you will be taken care of. Open up and focus on giving to the world rather than taking from it, trusting in it rather than trying to protect yourself from it.

Their teaching offers an alternative to power-over-others. Jesus and the Buddha lived in ways that challenged the conventional stories of their times and challenge just as much the dominant stories of our times. Despite hypocritical deference— the homage that other stories pay to this one—this message has had limited success. Yet it persists, with the potential to transform the world.

> Men are afraid to forget their minds, fearing to fall through
> the Void with nothing to stay their fall. They do not know
> that the Void is not really void, but the realm of the real Dharma.
> **Huangpo**

Our *no-thing-ness* is not really nothingness, for in that ground-lessness is the ground we seek.

To study the buddha way is to study yourself;
to study yourself is to forget yourself;
to forget yourself is to be actualized by myriad beings.
When actualized by myriad beings, your body and mind
as well as the bodies and minds of others drop away.

Dogen

The end of a life organized around fear is to forget your stories about yourself, and thereby your self.

As long as you do not know how to die and come to life again,
you are but a poor guest on this dark earth.

Goethe

The Big Stories

Let it be known there is a fountain

That was not made by the hands of men

The Grateful Dead

Big Stories are the overarching ones that explain everything, including our role within it. God is the best example, although scientism is a secular equivalent when "science can explain everything that can be explained."

Scientists generally agree on how to confirm or disprove their stories, for that is what distinguishes science from speculation. But how does one evaluate the Biggest Stories?

God is a unique narrative device: he creates his own stories, not being inside any bigger one. God is the story that trumps all others because the whole cosmos is within it. His story puts limitations on our own but there is the security of knowing that he controls all stories.

God is thus the guarantee that life has meaning. That our stories are meaningful.

We want to believe that there is a transcendent plot, an all-encompassing storyline that makes sense of everything, that will (or can) have a happy ending.

Essential to the God story is the denial that it is a story.

If triangles believed in God,
He would have three sides.
Yiddish proverb

Do we need a Story of Everything, to identify with and place ourselves within? The Buddha told a parable about a foolish man shot by a poisoned arrow, who insists on learning who shot the arrow, what his caste is, what the arrow is made of, and so forth, before he will allow anyone to pull it out.

The Dharma is a raft for ferrying across the river of samsara, not a Big Story to be carried on our backs everywhere we go.

In Mahayana Buddhism the *bodhisattva* is a buddha-in-training, whose final practice involves overcoming the remnants of self-preoccupation by self-lessly helping others. How should we understand this archetype? I can appeal to Kwan-yin, the celestial bodhisattva of compassion, when in need; or I can try to live as a bodhisattva myself.

There is a similar tension in Christianity between the belief that Jesus saves us and the importance of emulating his example.

Stories about God the Father, "the Lord," provide a model for power-over, legitimizing other top-down stories: popes, kings, fathers, husbands. The one atop the social pyramid has a unique relationship with God, playing a special role in the Biggest Story.

> Societies with social classes are significantly more likely
> than others to possess a belief in superior gods.
>
> **Guy E. Swanson**

Spiritual totalitarianism: only one Big Story is permitted. "I am the only God and you shall have no others." Other Big Stories co-exist or merge. A profusion of gods and myths overlap in India, while the Chinese tradition keeps syncretizing its different religious narratives.

New types of Big Stories developed in the Axial Age (during the first millennium BCE), involving a stronger sense of transcendence and therefore a greater sense of alienation between (ourselves in) this world and that which transcends it (God, Brahman, the *Logos*). To overcome this separation, personal and social transformation is needed. Religions became more egalitarian and individualistic: the transcendent does not relate to this world only through the top of the social hierarchy. The sacred can be discovered and cultivated within each of us.

The second awakening of the self is the discovery within us of the demand for the infinite, for the absolute. Once discovered, it is irresistible; it must be lived out. Its living out changes the meaning of everything we had experienced before. The second awakening is therefore a revolution in the experience of consciousness.

Roberto Unger

The problematic aspect of Axial stories is a greater dualism between the spiritual and the natural world/flesh/sexuality/women, the lower devalued as resistant to our higher nature. Bleeding women (menstruation, childbirth) remind us of something we would rather forget, that we are born and die like other animals.

Zoroaster, the first Axial revolutionary we know about, introduces new plot elements: a final apocalyptic war between Light and Dark, resurrection of the dead, the last judgment, heaven and hell. This new type of Big Story *ethicized* the old "combat myths" of heroes fighting monsters to wrest order from chaos. The Abrahamic religions emphasize being good, in contrast to nondualist traditions such as Buddhism, Vedanta, and Taoism, which emphasize realizing something.

The world is a battleground between Good and Evil and it is the duty of everyone to foster good and fight evil.

Zoroaster

Greece discovered the transcendent *Logos*. Early Greek philosophy distinguished reason from superstition yet still appreciated its own divine origins. Modern philosophy is embarrassed by Socrates' *daimon* because it has a more constricted understanding of rationality and what types of storying are valid. Yet there are many reason-able ways to story.

Today our exposure to so many religions creates new possibilities. As they rub against each other like stones in a tumbling machine, their Big Stories are challenged to distinguish what is essential from what is incidental.

Are we on the cusp of a new Big Story about Big Stories?

The main religious tension is not between religions—those open to dialogue get along well enough—but between the liberals and literals within each faith. Although they may agree on the important stories they understand them differently. The problem is greatest for those who identify with the Biggest Stories as (they suppose them to have been) understood in the past. The naturalness and inevitability of a Big Story cannot be recovered once it has been recognized as one among many.

Fundamentalists believe they are returning to the origins because they reconstruct the past in ways that deny its constructedness. Clinging harder to the "same" stories makes them different. We cannot avoid understanding them differently because we are different.

To suppose that the importance of the Bible depends on its historical truth is to argue like a fundamentalist. What matters and what has been preserved in it is its function as scripts for a drama. It offers stories that everyone can take part in. It provides a stage where we can find ourselves.

Richard C. Foltz

Like other stories, religious stories offer variations of previous ones. The Buddha's awakening under a pipal tree is usually presented as self-generated and self-authenticating, yet Buddhism inevitably incorporated older Vedic and shamanic stories about suffering, craving, karma, rebirth, and enlightenment.

Without a foundation in the conventional truth,
The significance of the ultimate truth cannot be taught.
Without understanding the significance of the ultimate truth,
Liberation is not achieved.

Nagarjuna

A Zen master slaps a student: "Just *this*!" Although the words try to reveal an ultimate truth by self-negating, they do not escape their conventional lower-truth-ness, which means that their value is instrumental. Realizing this relativity frees us from the grip of any particular religious story.

There is a positive side to what psychotherapy calls transference, for it is how we construct the larger reality needed to discover and develop ourselves. We project in order to be inspired by our projections.

> Projection is a necessary unburdening of the individual;
> man cannot live closed in upon himself and for himself.
> **Otto Rank**

Zen cannot be taught. When Zen students are inspired by their teachers, that teacher is, at least in part, an externalization of their own higher motivations.

> Man projects his nature into the world outside
> of himself before he finds it in himself.
> **Ludwig Feuerbach**

The transference must eventually be broken. The master, too, has feet of clay. If students have matured in their practice, by then they have realized their own "Buddha nature that is no nature." This "takes the problems of self-justification and removes it from the objects near at hand. We no longer have to please those around us, but the very source of creation" (Ernest Becker).

We know little about the historical Jesus, which makes it easy to project onto him our deepest aspirations. The source of creation embodied as a fellow human being who is not seduced by money or fame or power; who emphasizes loving one's neighbor, especially those who need that love the most; who is willing to suffer and die for us; who empties himself completely in order to become a vehicle for the cosmic process, thereby modeling what each of us needs to do.

How much of this myth is factual? Jesus as an archetype is no less a model. Christians believe that those who try to live in such a way are assisted by something greater than themselves. The love I attempt to embody is something that I find myself participating in. Then is the Christian story more than a story? Or a story that works in a special way?

The literary language of the New Testament is not intended, like literature itself, simply to suspend judgment, but to convey a vision of spiritual life that continues to transform and expand our own. That is, its myths become, as purely literary myths cannot, myths to live by; its metaphors become, as purely literary metaphors cannot, metaphors to live in.

Northrop Frye

The heart of the Buddha story is searching for insight into our true nature. His quest reminds me not to repress awareness of the suffering and death that haunt my life, but to let that awareness motivate my search for the meaning of life and death. The understanding needed is not conceptual but part of a holistic transformation that emphasizes letting go of the sense-of-self that feels separate from the world. The fruit of the Buddhist path is a freedom serene and empowered because not preoccupied with securing a self that cannot be secured.

Enlightenment is liberation from the dross of learning and experience that, without being aware of it, has accumulated and settled like so much sediment—or like cholesterol into one's arteries! It is the vivid, lively manifestation of the heart with which one is born—the heart that is no-form, no-mind, nonabiding, attached neither to form nor to thought, but in dynamic motion. Consequently, enlightenment is not an endpoint, but rather a place to start.

Soko Morinaga

My explanations are stories about the Jesus and Buddha stories. We do not have access to original events before interpretation; we choose from different narratives about those events. Bringing these Big Stories together helps to identify what remains important in each. Are they complementary?

Is this perspective more Buddhist than Christian? We never achieve a neutral standpoint outside all stories from which to evaluate them objectively.

Those who do not care for such Big Stories need to consider the alternative. There is no such thing as not storying. Everybody stories. The only choice we get is how to story.

In the day-to-day trenches of adult life, there is no such thing as atheism. There is no such thing as not worshipping. Everybody worships. The only choice we get is what to worship. And an outstanding reason for choosing some sort of god or spiritual-type thing to worship—be it JC or Allah, be it Yahweh or the Wiccan mother-goddess or the Four Noble Truths or some intangible set of ethical principles—is that pretty much anything else you worship will eat you alive. If you worship money and things—if they are where you tap real meaning in life—then you will never have enough. Never feel you have enough. Worship your own body and beauty and sexual allure and you will always feel ugly, and when time and age start showing, you will die a million deaths before they finally plant you. . . . Worship power—you will feel weak and afraid, and you will need ever more power over others to keep the fear at bay. Worship your intellect, being seen as smart—you will end up feeling stupid, a fraud, always on the verge of being found out.

The insidious thing about these forms of worship is not that they're evil or sinful; it is that they are unconscious. They are default settings. They're the kind of worship you just gradually slip into, day after day, getting more and more selective about what you see and how you measure value without ever being fully aware that that's what you're doing. And the world will not discourage you from operating on your default settings, because the world of men and money and power hums along quite nicely on the fuel of fear and contempt and frustration and craving and the worship of self. . . . The really important kind of freedom involves attention, and awareness, and discipline, and effort, and being able truly to care about other people and to sacrifice for them, over and over,

in myriad petty little unsexy ways, every day. That is real
freedom. The alternative is unconsciousness, the default
setting, the "rat race"—the constant gnawing sense
of having had and lost some infinite thing.

David Foster Wallace

Absolutely unmixed attention is prayer.

Simone Weil

Attentiveness is the natural prayer of the soul.

Nicolas Malebranche

Buddhism as Path of Failure

Although Shakyamuni Buddha's life is usually mythologized as
the predictable destiny of a spiritual conqueror, is he better
understood as a *failure*? He practiced this way and that, but
could not find what he was looking for: that which enabled
him to stop looking. Did he finally give up and just sit down?

I look for the form of awareness—the thought, perception, sen-
sation, etc.—that will liberate me, but liberation is *from*
attachment to any particular form, so no form that is grasped

can provide what I seek from it: a non-dwelling awareness that does not grasp.

We try to grasp something in a story that cannot be found in a story.

Let your mind come forth without fixing it anywhere.

Diamond Sutra

According to the Platform Sutra of Huineng, "When our mind works freely without any hindrance, and is at liberty to come or to go, we attain liberation." Such a mind "is everywhere present, yet it sticks nowhere."

Huineng had no system of Dharma to transmit: "What I do to my disciples is to liberate them from their own bondage with such devices as the case may need."

If you are fully aware in yourself of a non-dwelling mind, you will discover that there is just the fact of dwelling, with nothing to dwell upon or not to dwell upon. This full awareness in yourself of a mind dwelling upon nothing is known as having a clear perception of your own mind, or, in other words, as having a clear perception of your own nature. A mind which dwells upon nothing is the Buddha-mind, the mind of one already delivered, Bodhi-Mind, Un-created Mind...

Huihai

If you meet the Buddha, kill him. To meet someone who is a buddha is to distinguish buddhas from non-buddhas. Enlightenment-versus-delusion is a wonderful story that eventually self-negates.

> There is no specifiable difference whatever
> between nirvana and samsara.
> The limit of nirvana is the limit of samsara.
> There is not even the subtlest difference between the two.
> **Nagarjuna**

When I get a grip on the world, the world gets a grip on me.

> My propositions are elucidatory in this way: he who understands me finally recognizes them as senseless, when he has climbed out through them, on them, over them. He must, so to speak, throw away the ladder, after he has climbed up on it.
> **Wittgenstein**

Awareness is a bird that flies around picking up a leaf here, a twig there—a habit, an opinion—and weaves them into a nest. Instead of flying freely, the bird becomes obsessed with improving its nest. It always seems to need more attention.

The Zen tradition soon amassed the largest collection of Buddhist texts in China. That accumulating literature became the impetus for developing koans, which use those stories to free us from stories. "A special transmission outside the stories" is another story about getting rid of stories, but as a *practice* ...

Koans work because we get stuck in them and can get unstuck only by storying the situation differently. Does that mean a new story, or a new way of storying?

Imagining Liberation, Liberating Imagination

To be created in God's image is to partake in his creativity.

God brought the animals for Adam to name. Human creativity is grounded in language, which creates order out of chaos. In the beginning was the Word that includes our words.

God needs us as much as we need God. We need God because we are God's stories. God needs us because we are God's way to make new kinds of stories.

For Jakob Boehme man is the mirror-image of God because we share the power of divine imagination, which "transmutes us into an image of Christ; or rather the soul 'imagines into

Christ' while God, in turn, 'imagines into the soul'. Finally, imagination has the paradoxical power to carry us beyond all its images, including God, to the ineffable *Ungrund*, the formless unity of the 'God beyond God'" (Patrick Harpur).

> If there is no sense that the mythological universe is a human creation, man can never get free of servile anxieties and superstitions.... But, if there is no sense that it is also something uncreated, something coming from elsewhere, man remains a Narcissus staring at his own reflection.
>
> **Northrop Frye**

After eating from the tree of knowledge of good and evil, the eyes of Adam and Eve are opened and they cover their nakedness with leaves. God had told Adam he would die when he ate that fruit, but they do not die. Did God lie?

Becoming self-conscious is becoming aware of the death that haunts life. To become self-aware is to find oneself outside the Garden.

> The fall in Genesis is a fall into an objective nature, a creation in which we have not participated. The awakened imagination must "decreate" this fallen world in order to become itself a participant in creation.
>
> **Northrop Frye**

The fall into subjectivity is also a fall into objectivity: we discover ourselves to be in the world, not of it.

New species began to evolve. Taming fire led to cooked food, hot water, burnt offerings, torches to illuminate the night, metal tools, weapons. We till, plant, weed, harvest crops; make clothes, knives, spears, songs, poems; construct walls and gates, roads and bridges, boats, oars, sails, and fishing nets...

We are the image of God because our creativity is not other than God's. If sense of self is itself a creation—if my sense of self is not *my* sense of self—how could it be otherwise?

> The eye I see God with is the eye God sees me with: my eye and
> God's eye are one eye, one seeing, one knowing and one love.
> **Meister Eckhart**

> The soul's vision of its divine Lord is
> the vision which He has of the soul.
> **Ibn 'Arabi**

Is evolution random and meaningless? Even 13.8 billion years seems a short time to develop from Big Bang plasma to the fusion of higher elements (in the cores of stars) enabling the natural selection of self-replicating species, and then the cultural evolution necessary to produce a Buddha or a Gandhi. Is this groping self-organization the process by which the cosmos is becoming aware of itself?

If my awareness is not *my* awareness, is my desire to awaken the urge of the cosmos to awaken in and as me?

> God is closer to me than I am to myself.
>
> **Augustine**

Every species is an experiment of the biosphere, and less than one percent of those experiments still survive today. Our super-sized cortex makes us co-creators, but something has gone wrong with our hyper-rationality. Are we viable only as a transitional species? Must we evolve further in order to survive at all? If the delusion of separate self means we are haunted by too much *dukkha* "dis-ease"—which makes us self-destructive—figures like the Buddha and Jesus may be harbingers of how we collectively need to develop.

> Man is a rope stretched between the animal and the superman—
> a rope over an abyss. A dangerous crossing, a dangerous wayfaring,
> a dangerous looking-back, a dangerous trembling and halting.
>
> **Nietzsche**

Perhaps the basic problem isn't self-love but misunderstanding what self is. Without the compassion that arises from realizing our nonduality—empathy not only with other humans but with the planet—civilization as we know it may not outlive this century. Nor would it deserve to. It remains to be seen whether the *Homo sapiens* experiment will be a successful vehicle for the cosmic evolutionary process.

> The universe is the only self-referential reality in the phenomenal world. It is the only text without context. Everything else has to be seen in the context of the universe…
> The universe story is the quintessence of reality.
> **Thomas Berry**

The Abrahamic traditions emphasize that *God must not be imaged or named.* If "God" is the source of images, the wellspring of creative Imagination, to give God any name or form is to deny his essential formlessness, his *no-thing-ness.*

Idolatry is mistaking representations of the divine for the divine. Images, dogmas, rituals, institutions, etc. become idols when used to grasp what cannot be grasped. Concepts become idolatrous when employed to conceive of that which cannot be conceived.

The best stories are paradoxical, one hand offering what the other takes back.

Has anyone at the end of the nineteenth century a clear idea
of what poets of strong ages have called *inspiration*? . . .
If one had the slightest residue of superstition left in one's
system, one could hardly reject altogether the idea that one
is merely incarnation, merely mouthpiece, merely a medium
of overpowering forces. The concept of *revelation*—in a sense
that suddenly, with indescribable certainty and subtlety, something
becomes visible, audible, something that shakes one to the last
depths and throws one down—that merely describes the facts.
One hears, one does not seek; one accepts, one does not ask
who gives; like lightning, a thought flashes up, with necessity,
without hesitating regarding its form—I never had any choice. . . .
Everything happens involuntarily in the highest degree
but as in a gale of a feeling of freedom,
of absoluteness, of power, of divinity.

Nietzsche

While drawing, I feel as if I were a spiritualistic medium,
controlled by the creatures that I am conjuring up, and it is as if
they themselves decide on the shape in which they like to appear.

M. C. Escher

According to Swedenborg we are in heaven right now, if we are
receptive to the divine influx.

I heard, and I wrote what I heard. I am the vessel
through which *The Rite of Spring* passed.

Stravinsky

Madame Butterfly was dictated to me by God:
I was merely instrumental in putting it on paper
and communicating it to the public.

Puccini

Socrates in the *Phaedrus* says that "our greatest blessings come
to us by way of madness [*mania*]," provided that "the madness
is given to us by divine gift."

I don't write what I want. . . . I don't choose my subjects
or plots. They are given to me. I have to stand back
and receive them in a passive moment.

Jorge Luis Borges

I have written this poem ["Milton"] from immediate dictation
twelve or sometimes even twenty or thirty lines at a time,
without premeditation and even against my will.

William Blake

For William Blake *Imagination is Eternity*. "I know of no other Christianity than the liberty both of body and mind to exercise the Divine Arts of Imagination . . . Is the Holy Ghost any other than an Intellectual Fountain? . . . What are the Gifts of the Gospel? Are they not all Mental [Imaginative] Gifts?"

The imagination is "the Divine Body of the Lord Jesus" and "Man is all Imagination. God is Man & exists in us & we in him."

Literature is the Imaginal in script.

Northrop Frye

"I feel as if I was inside a song, if you get my meaning."

Sam Gamgee, in *The Lord of the Rings*

If the Big Story of Buddhism is not to be deluded by storying, the Big Story for William Blake is the storying of liberated Imagination. Are these different stories, or two sides of a Bigger Story?

Imagination is more important than knowledge. . . . When I examine myself and my methods of thought, I come to the conclusion that the gift of imagination has meant more to me than my talent for absorbing absolute knowledge.

Albert Einstein

"Yes, it is true," said the Childlike Empress, and her golden
eyes darkened. "All lies were once creatures of Fantastica.
They are made of the same stuff—but they have lost their
true nature and become unrecognizable. . . . Every human
who has been here has learned something that could be
learned only here, and returned to his own world a changed
person. Because he had seen you creatures in your true form,
he was able to see his own world and his fellow humans with
new eyes. Where he had seen only dull, everyday reality,
he now discovered wonders and mysteries. . . . And the more
these visits enriched our world, the fewer lies there were
in theirs, the better it became. Just as our two worlds can injure
each other, they can also make each other whole again."

Michael Ende, *The Neverending Story*

When meditating one dwells in the empty, silent *no-thing-ness*
from which mental phenomena arise; when thoughts and
images appear one lets them go. The creators quoted above are
more interested in what arises from that *no-thing-ness*.

If form is emptiness and emptiness is form, does *no-thing-ness* delight in the productions of the Imagination?

The East emphasizes liberation from the human condition,
while the Western spiritual traditions place special value
on the human incarnation in its own right, and are more
interested in fulfilling the meaning of this incarnation than

in going beyond it or in finding release from it. . . . To bring
these two together is an important evolutionary step.

John Welwood

The esoteric practices of tantric Buddhism work to develop and liberate the Imagination. One common meditation involves visualizing awakened beings. As light flows from those luminous beings and penetrates us, we merge with them, embodying their serenity, wisdom, and compassion. We imagine that we are what we would like to be. Sense of self is deconstructed and reconstructed into an enlightened being.

One concludes by dissolving the whole imaginary panorama into emptiness.

When you imagine things . . . they start to grow.
If you love them, they love you back.

Michelle, New York City schoolchild

The Christian heaven, the Pure Land of Buddhism: are we suddenly whisked away to them, or do we gain them by becoming the kind of person who would live in such a place?

The world is made of stories. Good stories are hard to come by,
and a good story you can honestly call your own
is an incredible gift. These stories are part of
a bigger story that connects us all.

Gary Snyder

If the world is made of stories, who knows what our best stories might accomplish? If we ourselves are Buddha, who but us can create the Pure Land?

Hope is like a road in the country;
there was never a road,
but when many people walk on it,
the road comes into existence.

Lin Yutang

Acknowledgments

Thanks as always to the fine folk at Wisdom Publications, especially Josh Bartok for his tactful efforts to focus my meandering thoughts, and Laura Cunningham for her careful editing.

Thanks also to Linda, for taking care of me and putting up with me, and to our son Mark, who has begun to live his own stories.

The Brian Andreas poem on page 16 is reprinted with the kind permission of Brian Andreas, Storypeople.

Index

About the Author

 David R. Loy's previous books include *Non-duality: A Study in Comparative Philosophy*; *Lack and Transcendence: The Problem of Death and Life in Psychotherapy*; *Existentialism and Buddhism*; *A Buddhist History of the West: Studies in Lack*; *The Great Awakening: A Buddhist Social Theory*; the bestselling *Money, Sex, War, Karma: Notes for a Buddhist Revolution*; *Awareness Bound and Unbound: Buddhist Essays*; and (with Linda Goodhew) *The Dharma of Dragons and Daemons: Buddhist Themes in Modern Fantasy*, a finalist for the 2006 Mythopoeic Scholarship Award. He is also the editor of *Healing Deconstruction: Postmodern Thought in Buddhism and Christianity* and co-editor of *A Buddhist Response to the Climate Emergency*.

A Zen practitioner for many years, he is qualified as a teacher in the Sanbo Kyodan tradition of Japanese Zen Buddhism.

About Wisdom Publications

Wisdom Publications, a nonprofit publisher, is dedicated to making available authentic works relating to Buddhism for the benefit of all. We publish books by ancient and modern masters in all traditions of Buddhism, translations of important texts, and original scholarship. Additionally, we offer books that explore East-West themes unfolding as traditional Buddhism encounters our modern culture in all its aspects. Our titles are published with the appreciation of Buddhism as a living philosophy, and with the special commitment to preserve and transmit important works from Buddhism's many traditions.

To learn more about Wisdom, or to browse books online, visit our website at www.wisdompubs.org.

You may request a copy of our catalog online or by writing to this address:

Wisdom Publications
199 Elm Street
Somerville, Massachusetts 02144 USA

Telephone: 617-776-7416
Fax: 617-776-7841
Email: info@wisdompubs.org
www.wisdompubs.org

The Wisdom Trust

As a nonprofit publisher, Wisdom is dedicated to the publication of Dharma books for the benefit of all sentient beings and dependent upon the kindness and generosity of sponsors in order to do so. If you would like to make a donation to Wisdom, you may do so through our website or our Somerville office. If you would like to help sponsor the publication of a book, please write or email us at the address above.

Thank you.

Wisdom is a nonprofit, charitable 501(c)(3) organization affiliated with the Foundation for the Preservation of the Mahayana Tradition (FPMT).